D1484349

STOLEN Childhood

Coming of age while surviving the Holocaust

Nathan Taffel's Life Story by Keri Guten Cohen

Printed in Canada

First Printing, 2010
Second Printing, 2011
Third Printing, 2015
ISBN 978-0-578-05953-2

Heart Printing & Graphics
7223 Blythdale Drive
Dallas TX 75248

Ordering information: www.nathantaffel.com

This book is dedicated
to the memory
of Nathan Taffel's
beloved family members
who perished during the Holocaust.
He thinks of them every day.

Acknowledgments

I wish to express my gratitude to Muriel and Nate Taffel, who flew me numerous times to Florida and Milwaukee for interview and editing sessions, and who were understanding about how long this project has taken.

I also am very grateful to my friend and colleague at the *Detroit Jewish News*, Deborah Schultz, who expressed interest in this memoir and who used her considerable talent to make it look so meaningful and so much more personal than a regular book. Her design of these pages features the motif of leaves, signifying the passage of time and seasons. Placed at the beginning of the chapters, a single symbolic leaf progresses from colorful and cheery in Nate's happy early childhood to brown and decaying during his Holocaust years, then progressively back to colorful and blooming as Nate gains freedom and moves on throughout his wonderful life with his family.

Several people helped with the editing of this book, including my mother, Miriam Guten; my brother-in-law Artie Moskowitz (who also arranged for the printing); my husband Don Cohen; and my friend and fellow professional journalist Karen Schwartz.

Thanks, too, to Jeff Meyer for his help with the photos and to the unknown photographhter who shot the cover photo of Nate at age 17½ shortly after liberation.

My thanks to you all for your support and invaluable help.

Keri Guten Cohen
June 2010

Introduction

My Uncle Nate and I have been close since I was a child. He's always done amusing things: told jokes, teased me, sang silly songs I remember to this day, beat me mercilessly at cards and slipped me $20 every now and then when no one was looking — all with a smile and a blink of those baby blue eyes.

He also has a serious side, but he doesn't show it as often. I knew he was a Holocaust survivor, but it didn't really sink in until I was a teenager. For an English class, I was assigned to do an in-depth interview with someone, then turn it into a narrative.

The assignment coincided with a family trip from Dallas to Milwaukee to see relatives, so I decided to corner Nate for an interview. To my surprise, he said yes. During that visit, the two of us took long, slow walks in a nearby park. I asked a few questions and he talked. He didn't reveal everything, but I think the talking – and the walking — was good for both of us. That's when I first learned about his "stolen childhood," and I started to understand what shaped this man who is my uncle.

Perhaps his oldest son, Craig, who is very much like his father, sums it up best.

"When I think of my father, one word comes to mind: survivor. My father is a survivor in every sense of the word. Life does not always deal us a great hand of cards. Sometimes we lose; sometimes we win. My father has seen some of the worst cards that life can deal, but rather than admitting defeat, he has taken his losses and learned from them. He has taken his losses and shared his knowledge with others so they, too, can learn.

"It is funny, in life, how we seem to remember the negative more clearly. Not my father. He has always accentuated the positive. For those of us who know him well, we know that one of his great joys is to take a bad hand and turn it in his favor. There is no better feeling than to sit back, look at the cards life has dealt you and be able to say, GIN!"

1

Persistent Memories

Nathan Taffel is a man of memories. Some have been too painful to utter out loud until only recently, but he'll tell you their flickering presence has been with him every day since childhood.

Like a tragic movie, these memories are vivid reminders of the most precious loss one can endure — that of family. Robbed of childhood by the Nazi Holocaust during World War II and saved twice by miracles, Nate relies on memories to fill in the past, while he lives in today's world with his wife, Muriel, their three children and two grandchildren. The memories, though, are never far from his mind.

"I would like to go back to my childhood, before the atrocity to my family and the Jewish people," he says. "It's very important to tell you about my family. It's very seldom that I don't think about them. Holidays, family occasions bring out memories, reminders that I didn't get a chance to grow up with my parents."

Before the war, Naftali Taffel was a happy child. Born on May 17, 1928, the youngest of 10 children, the curly-haired boy with the bright blue eyes was spoiled by his loving parents and his siblings. He remembers a joyous home in Poland amid an Orthodox Jewish family that celebrated each holiday with gusto.

"Everyone came home to be together," he said, recalling his sisters Rifcia, twins Rochel and Shaindl, Gittel, Sima, Tobah and Faiga and his brother Leon. Eldest brother Jochinam moved to Argentina when Nate was a baby.

His doting mother, Mindel, would cook three or four dishes at mealtimes, just to please her fussy children. She had a way

This is the only family portrait that exists of the whole Taffel family in Poland. Nate is sitting on his mother's lap. Circa 1930.

of making every child feel he or she was Mother's favorite. To Nate, she was the most loving person in the world. She called him Tulek, a common nickname for Naftali.

When Nate was very young, his family and both sets of grandparents lived on land they owned and farmed outside the Polish town of Radomysl Wielki (pronounced *Radom-ish Vi-elki*). But, with seven daughters and few Jewish young men living out in the country, Nate's father, Avram Chaim, decided to move his large family into town. He opened a grain exchange on the bottom floor of a two-story building directly on the square. His wife was a great help in the business, along with second son, Leibisch, later known as Leon.

A grain exchange made sense for business because Radomysl Wielki was known for its flour milling and brickworks. The small town is in south central Poland about 60 miles east of Krakow, in what is known as the Kolbuszowa region. Before the war, the area was made up of neighboring *shtetlach,* villages where Jews came together through marriage and commerce and because they shared such basic elements as cemeteries, schools, kosher butchers and bakers. The larger shtetl nearby was Mielec, which served as the administrative hub of the region.

Every Thursday, the farmers brought their produce to the town square. They also brought livestock, fish and chicken. Products were bought by Jews and gentiles alike. Nate remembers his maternal grandfather, Lazar Amsterdam, sending produce from the farm to his family. Nate's uncle, who was also a farmer, sent various types of produce as well.

Nate remembers that he had a forester cousin who brought dead animals to sell for their fur on the square. "He had them in a bag," Nate said, "and I refused to open the bag because I was too frightened to see what was inside."

Before the Holocaust, nearly 1,500 Jews lived in Radomysl Wielki, which was founded in 1581. It is believed that Jews existed there for as many as 14 generations or about 360 years. Jewish life continued to be rich in the days when Naftali was a young boy.

The Taffels lived in an apartment behind their large grain store. On the building's second floor were apartments occupied by a rabbi, a Hebrew teacher, a tailor, a police sergeant and a *shmata* (used clothing) salesman. Nate has vivid memories of the store and his parents' apartment.

"The kitchen was so large I could drive a bike around the table," he said. "The bedroom was behind the kitchen and the kitchen had beds in it. The bedroom was large and was used by my sisters and brother. I was the youngest, so I slept with my parents. In the winter, I slept in the bedroom with my sisters. Some nights in the winter it was so cold and the wind was blowing so hard, I became frightened. Then I would end up with my parents again. I was very spoiled."

This was a loving family, where doting on the youngest just made sense. This also was a family that was in pretty good shape financially. Friday night Shabbat meals often included those less fortunate.

"On Shabbos, my father closed the store early," he said. "We took some food, like *cholent* (a traditional dish that Nate's mother made with ground potatoes and meat), to the bakery to cook in the ovens over Shabbos. My mother worked very hard. She baked bread at home and had to have an animal – a calf or a chicken – ritually killed. Then we brought it home to pluck or clean."

In those days, everything was done by hand. Nate's grandparents would bring butter and vegetables in from their farm. In the summer, there were a variety of cheeses, milk and breads. In the winter, more meat was eaten and cooked foods were taken to a special shed filled with ice from the river. Women saved rainwater in tubs so they could do laundry. A vendor sold drinking water that was stored in the house in a bucket. Lunch was the biggest meal and everyone sat down together.

Nate remembers three synagogues in Radomysl Wielki. Only one of them leaned toward the more liberal Reform end of the spectrum, and he recalls hearing that some people weren't so kosher there. His synagogue was very Orthodox.

Nate's best friend, Shimek, was more Reform and not too kosher, so Nate's parents weren't too happy about the friendship. They told him he could not eat at Shimek's house.

One Rosh Hashanah as a young child, Nate was sent to the tailor for a new suit. "I was very excited," he said. "It was short pants and a jacket. The holidays were very happy. My sisters and their spouses would come. I remember that Gittel and Moshe arrived in a taxi. I was 9 or 10, and it was the first time I saw a car. All the kids came to see it. The only other vehicle in town was a bus."

At that time, Radomysl Wielki had no newspapers nor any radios. Nate's oldest brother-in-law, Mendel, would get a Jewish newspaper from another city once a week. People relied on local gossip.

"One little lady named 'Yenta' would tell the news and it would spread fast among the Jews," Nate said.

As the youngest, Nate had many pets — a dog, pigeons and a porcupine that frightened him. His father would pick it up with a handkerchief to keep from getting pricked by the animal's barbs. For a while, there was a cow in the back yard; but his father sold it to a man for some tobacco. "My mother was very unhappy; she didn't want my father to smoke," Nate said. "Every morning he would cough."

Nate also remembers some of the old superstitions from when he was a carefree youngster. In the summer, he remembers playing with rare golden spotted ladybugs. He used to let them run over his hands and play with them. In Yiddish, they were called *moshiachlicht,* or Messiahs, so parents told the children not to kill them. When they took off, it was said "the Messiah had left." Excited, Nate would try to run home to show his parents the *moshichl,* but they'd always fly away.

Because there were so many sisters, weddings happened often in the big kitchen in the house in Radomsyl Wielki. Invitations were issued verbally or sent by mail, and someone checked the list at the door to limit the amount of people. The men were eating and dancing in one room, the women in the other. The cooking took days and days. Nate remembers participating in the weddings of four of his sisters. Matchmakers had arranged them all.

"Every daughter got 10 hectares of land as a dowry," Nate said. "I remember one brother-in-law was not successful, so my father gave them another 10 hectares of land. My oldest sister, Rifcia, who didn't live far away in town, had a child about two years younger than I was. Yossel and I would play often until they moved to Tarnow."

2

Anti-Semitic Rumblings

Nate attended Hebrew school four nights a week as well as public school in Radomysl Wielki. The public school was right next door to his house. He was a good student, curious and interested in learning. For the most part, he had good experiences at school, but he also remembers incidents of anti-Semitism from Polish classmates before World War II.

"The kids knew I was Jewish," Nate said. "I practiced *kashruth* (keeping kosher). More students were non-Jewish, and there was a lot of anti-Semitism. I was pointed out as 'You, Jew.' I was hit and got into fights. In class, a gentile kid took away my papers and tore them up. The teacher ignored it and showed bias against me."

Nate explains that the Jewish kids were a minority and teachers were not Jewish, so there was not too much emphasis placed on educating the Jewish students.

"Now I felt more than ever that we were living as foreigners or second-class citizens. Our citizenship papers said, 'Descendants of Moses.' "

He remembers much of the trouble surrounded holidays —Jewish and non-Jewish.

"On Sukkot, the gentiles would throw stones into our sukkah. After Easter, Polish people came out and beat Jewish kids for crucifying Jesus. They broke windows," he said.

Being the youngest of so many, Nate was sheltered from much of the persecution.

"I was very protected," he recalled. "I asked my parents questions about why the gentiles didn't like us, but they would say to just ignore them. They didn't go into the details of hate or anti-Semitism. They didn't want me to have fear."

Still, Nate would overhear his parents and their friends talking about politics. They'd say the old prime minister was good to Jews, for example, while the new one was anti-Semitic.

"My parents were fearful," Nate said, with the hindsight of an adult. Looking back, he sees now how the Jews often were scapegoats for misfortune that befell the townspeople.

"When crops were poor, Jews were blamed for their failure," Nate said. "Jews created a drought. There really was no other race or religion they could blame except the Jews. They never let you forget you were Jewish."

3

War Rushes In

War broke out in 1939. Poland soon was occupied by Nazi soldiers and the anti-Semitism intensified.

Nate vividly remembers the day the Germans entered Radomysl Wielki. His large family hid in the basement of their house. Below ground, they could hear the soldiers marching in the streets because of the metal plates on the soles of their boots. Nate remembers that he and his father went upstairs first. His father greeted a soldier who, in turn, began beating him. This was the beginning of Nate's devastation.

He recalls, too, that not all gentiles rejoiced or escalated their animosity. Because he was so young at the time, he learned later from his brother-in-law that the family had a gentile man working for them who was willing to create a shelter to hide them. This kindhearted man named Juzek was close to the family. However, he only had a small house in the country, too small to conceal a family of eight or nine. Nate's father was very concerned not only about his family's survival, but also Juzek's. Juzek had many young children who might have talked about the hidden family. If his neighbors reported him, Juzek would have been killed, too.

In 1940, the Jews were constantly harassed. There was no more school for Jewish children. And Jews had to surrender all valuables, including furs and silver. Soldiers searched houses and took anything of value.

"We began burying things in the back yard: silver candlesticks, American money sent from relatives for birthdays and other occasions. I made the holes in the yard. I wonder if they are still there?" Nate said.

A typical shtetl with Jews identified by a yellow star.
Bundesarchiv/Wikimedia Commons

As the year wore on, conditions grew progressively worse. Because his Grandfather Lazar had a farm, Nate and his father left town to go work on the farm, which was a day's drive by horse and wagon. Nate was the shepherd for the cows. A curious, active child, he hated the job because it was so boring.

After a while, the farm no longer offered asylum. Gentiles began threatening Jewish farmers, who often were chased off their land, only to have their livestock, poultry and crops seized by these gentiles. Leaving everything behind, Nate and his father went back to Radomysl Wielki after similar threats were made to them.

When the Germans occupied Poland, Nate was around 11 years old, too young to wear the Star of David that identified all Jews who were 13 and older. In a town without a ghetto, this badge made it easier for the SS and Gestapo to beat up or kill Jews or to set fire to the men's long beards.

Wikimedia Commons

Often the Nazis would target different areas of town on various days; Nate remembers hearing the gunshots, sometimes closer, sometimes farther away.

The SS men, in their black uniforms and who often had Baltic and Ukrainian backgrounds, were extremely brutal. The Jews of Radomysl Wielki went into hiding to avoid them.

"On one occasion, the SS selected young Jewish men to help liquidate the Jews from the city. Their job was to bury some of the Jewish people from Radomysl Wielki whom the Germans had killed," Nate said. "My brother, Leon, was one of those chosen.

A young boy in Radom, Poland, distributes armbands that identify Jews with a yellow Jewish star.

Bundesarchiv/Wikimedia Commons

"I'll never forget that one day I drove my bike to the place where he was stationed. The Gestapo were picking Jews for execution. They yelled to me to stop, but I didn't do it immediately. So they took their pistols out of their holsters to shoot me. Miraculously, Leon saw this from the window and ran out and said, 'That's my brother.' He pleaded with them to let me go and they finally did. I didn't realize how close I was to being shot."

4

Realizing The New Reality

The day after Leon saved him from the Nazis, Nate observed many trucks with German SS soldiers in black uniforms and gray uniforms entering the center of town. One specific truck was an enclosed white van with a glass window in the rear. This one stood out more than the other open trucks. A year or so later, when Nate and his sisters were reunited with Leon in a camp in Mielec, he and his sisters learned that the truck was used to eliminate Jewish people who were old, feeble, mentally sick — and the babies. Leon told them these people were put inside the van and poisoned with carbon monoxide.

"On that same day the trucks came, my parents knew the destiny of the Jews of the city," Nate said, explaining that his parents understood the many soldiers were there to liquidate the city as part of Hitler's "final solution."

"The shooting and killing by the Gestapo happened constantly after the Occupation. The Nazis often came into town and randomly picked people to shoot, but my parents kept that away from me and my sister because we were very young," Nate said. "I tried to listen to the adults, but I could only pick up a few things. I felt a constant fear because I saw the expressions

A Nazi poster blames Jews for typhus. Wikimedia Commons

Nate's sister, Gittel, and her husband Moishe Presser.

of the adults. When we asked why they were so distraught, there was never really an answer. I was always on guard. I felt something drastic was happening, but I didn't understand why.

"Occasionally, German Jews ousted from Germany came to our town. They came into our house and the adults in my family gathered to hear about the atrocities happening in Germany and parts of Poland as well as about Jewish business owners being forced out. These German Jews were more informed because people in Radomysl had very few sources of information. Only one Jewish family owned a battery-operated radio, but the batteries didn't last long and that source of information disappeared."

Nate remembers the pervasive sadness in his family. From the time of occupation, he says, there were no joyous occasions to celebrate. Holidays were celebrated in a very subdued manner.

"I had three sisters — Shaindel, Rochel and Rifcia — who were married and living out of town in Mielec, Tarnow and Kranitz. Soon after the Occupation, I don't remember anybody talking about their destiny because there was no mail or communication. We didn't know what ever happened to them and their families at all. We think they were sent to the Treblinka gas chambers."

5

All Jews Out

Nate remembers conditions grew even worse as the war progressed. Emotions were close to the surface, no matter how hard people tried to submerge them. Nate recalls some Jewish people walked around crying all the time.

Against this emotional backdrop, Nate believes he is close to age 12. The traditional time for a Jewish boy to become a bar mitzvah (literally "son of the commandments" or a Jewish adult) is age 13, but these were extraordinary times and his parents knew the worst was coming. His father asked him to say certain prayers, then simply told him he was a bar mitzvah. No laughter. No joy.

"Growing up in a family where holidays were crowded and happy, this was abnormal," he said. "Because of the war, it was very sad, but my father felt it was important to tell me I had become a bar mitzvah."

Two days later, shortly after the SS arrived and his parents understood the atrocities awaiting the Jews in Radomysl, life would take a dramatic turn.

"That evening, my parents and my youngest sister Faiga and I went with a horse and wagon to the city of Tarnow, where my sister Rifcia, her husband Mendel and their son Yossel lived. It was a bigger city and they were already in the ghetto," Nate said. "I'm surmising today that my parents must have known the Germans would liquidate Radomysl.

"Leon and my three sisters, Tobah, Sima and Gittel, stayed in Radomysl. They stayed because they must have assumed that being young they might be saved by going to labor camps." As Nate sees it today, there was no rhyme or reason for their staying.

Nate and his sister Faiga left their home in Radomsyl on a horse and wagon similar to this one on their way to the Tarnow ghetto. Bundesarchiv/Wikimedia Commons

They just hoped they had a chance of survival there.

At age 19 or 20, Leon, who was part of the Jewish burial force, participated in the Radomysl liquidation.

"There were a lot of killings," Nate said he learned. "Leon never wanted to talk about it. Unknown to us until later on, he was sent to Mielec labor camp nearby, where his job was to bury the people the Germans were shooting during the elimination of the Jews of Radomysl. Leon threw dirt on the graves the Jews had to dig for themselves. As they were shot, they had to line up so they fell directly into those graves. Little babies were not shot, but they crushed their heads against the wall.

"Leon could not forget the crying and screaming from those people throughout his life. That experience, and more that followed, would haunt him for the rest of his life."

Nate's three sisters were separated from his brother. Tobah, Sima and Gittel, along with Gittel's husband, Moishe Presser, were sent from Radomysl to Smoczka, a German Army camp. They would be reunited with more siblings, but not before a devastating separation.

"After we'd been in Tarnow's ghetto for a period of time, there was a lot of talk between my parents and Rifcia and Mendel," Nate recalled. "One evening a gentleman comes in and Mendel put coats on my sister Faiga and me. I looked into my parents' room through a crack in the door. How did they feel about us

Ruins of the Jewish cemetery in Tarnow.
www.holocaustresearchproject.org

Laborers exhume Jewish bodies shot in a mass grave in Tarnow. www.holocaustresearchproject.org

being taken away? I wanted to say something, but Mendel knew what was happening and he rushed us out onto a truck. I never saw my parents again. I never even said goodbye. And we didn't know what would happen to us.

"It scares me to this day, and my emotions are very, very strong about this separation from my dear loved ones."

This wrenching experience helped shape the type of parent Nate would become later in life. A doting, loving father, he is close to his children and grandchildren. To this day, he talks to all three children daily, and keeps in close contact with his nieces and nephews.

Nate's sister, Rifcia, and her husband, Mendel Schweber (1938). Rifcia did not survive the gas chambers. Mendel survived the war and passed on information about the fate of many of Nate's family members.

When young Nate and his sister were ushered out of their sister's house in Tarnow, they were hoisted onto the back of a truck and covered with canvas. Mendel told them not to talk, cough or move — just to sit. The gentile driver, who was paid with valuables hidden by his sisters and brother-in-law, was stopped at the exit to the ghetto and asked if he had anything to declare.

"The Germans couldn't see us," Nate recalled. "My sister kept me very quiet — we didn't even breathe."

They were taken to the camp at Smoczka, where they were greeted by three very surprised sisters, who were amazed that their young siblings had been saved from the ghetto.

After the war, Nate learned from Mendel that his parents had been shot in the Tarnow ghetto, which was liquidated by the vicious German SS-Hauptsturmfuhrer Amon Goeth, commandant of the Plaszow concentration camp. Goeth, who was hanged in 1946 for his war crimes, was depicted in the film *Schindler's List.*

Rifcia and Yossel had been taken to Treblinka or Mjdanek. They did not survive the gas chambers.

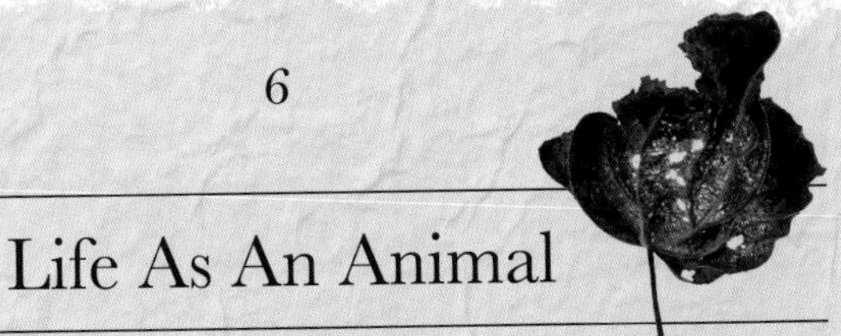

6

Life As An Animal

At 13, when he was supposed to be in school, having fun with boys his age, playing sports and preparing for his bar mitzvah, Nate says he started living like an animal. To survive, he did things he was told to do by the Germans and SS officers. He feels his older sisters knew more than they were telling, but he focused on survival.

In the camp, the men were separated from the women and all were fed horsemeat and other meager foodstuffs. A normal meal was bread with margarine and water. At lunch, they were given soup.

Because he was young, very strong and very diligent, Nate became a "go-fer" for the foreman of the road construction being done within the German camp in the city of Smozcka.

On occasion, Nate saw the Nazis take the old, young and disabled outside the camp. He heard shots, but was never told what had happened. One day a Gestapo officer pulled Nate into such a group. Miraculously, he was saved by the foreman, who told the officer that Nate was a good worker.

After the construction job was finished in Smozcka, the Jews were rounded up and taken to an unknown destination, which turned out to be the Mielec labor camp where there was an airplane factory run by the Germans.

There, amazingly, Nate was reunited with brother Leon, who was assigned to live in the same barracks.

At Mielec, Nate received the permanent blue tattoo on his right forearm that branded him as a victim — and survivor — of the Holocaust.

"They lined us up and everyone received a tattoo on our right arm that was a 'KL.' That stood for *Koncentration Lager* (concentration camp) and I think it also stood for SS man Karl Lundersdorf, commander of the camp. (Nate thinks this is the spelling of his name. As with some dates and names, Nate admits his memory may not be accurate because this all happened to him at such a young age.)

"They stretched the skin on our arm," Nate said, "then used the same sharp nail dunked in ink — one after the other. On my arm, the area got hard and swelled up. There was no doctor. Nature healed the deep wound."

On another day, those in the camp were lined up and German engineers and supervisors selected people for labor.

"I was strong, so I was picked to work in the transportation department, one of the worst places," Nate recalled. "We loaded and unloaded equipment needed for repairing airplanes. I also worked inside, cleaning offices and was a messenger. There were very few kids my age.

"The Jews I worked with were constantly beaten up because they didn't move fast enough or do the job of separating train cars fast enough. One foreman in particular, a Pole of German descent, especially enjoyed beating people up. On one occasion, the Jews were trying to move railroad carriages that were loaded and too heavy. He was beating people. Without thinking about the consequences, I went out to help by putting myself between the carriages to help move them. I really could have gotten in trouble, but I knew what I could do before I got hurt."

Those who worked in the factory had a worse situation. At least Nate was inside, away from the cold. Still, he says, they treated people like animals.

"I'm not sure about the adults, but as far as I was concerned, that's how it was supposed to be. As a teen, I didn't know any different. Mentally it had to be more difficult for the adults, who understood that the future was very bleak."

Fortunately, there were moments when human compassion was still evident, quietly but noticeably.

"Where I worked in the offices and buildings, they would leave me scraps of bread. I'd ask if I could have them and when there was no answer, it meant I could take it," he said. "One girl left extra bread on the crust – for me that was extra food."

Memorial to the Jews killed in Mielec.
shtetlinks.jewishgen.org

Life was unbearable in Mielec. In the barracks, people slept two to a bunk and had very little food. There were no showers, no doctors, no dentists. Any person with health problems rarely recovered. Most just passed away or were shot.

"I didn't grow. I was stunted," Nate explained. "I had toothaches. One dentist — a Jewish dentist working as a laborer — just pulled my tooth out with pliers. It is surprising to me today to realize how much pain a person can endure when they have no choice and think this is how it is supposed to be."

Jews were worked six days a week, from dawn until dusk, with only Sunday as a rest day.

"I was already geared to live like an animal," Nate said. "I got up, worked, then went to sleep. Young as I was, I don't remember talking about Jewish holidays. I knew Shabbos was the day before Sunday, but I was too young to realize the consequences of doing anything beyond routine. You knew every day you could die. And it didn't matter."

7

Destination Unknown

"One day in Mielec, all the males were gathered in the middle of the camp and loaded on a train," Nate remembered. "Our destination at that time was unknown. I was separated from my sisters, but still with Leon. We arrived in Wieliczka, a town just outside of Auschwitz. The camp was operating at capacity and there was no room for us."

After a few days in Wieliczka, the men were called together in the middle of the camp and the Germans made them strip naked. Nate found a gold coin on the ground and surrendered it to the SS so they wouldn't think he was hiding it. Then the Germans gave them gray-and-black striped uniforms, caps and wooden shoes. They lined people up and marked them with red ink. "T" on the forehead meant *tot*, German for dead. Another symbol indicated a work detail.

"My brother and I went to Flossenburg in Bavaria, Germany. This camp was originally for homosexuals and political prisoners. It had been converted into factories for repairing planes shot down by the Allies. The Jews had their own barracks."

Gray and black striped uniforms and wooden shoes were standard issue for Jews in camps.
Wikimedia Commons

Flossenburg was a small camp, not meant for many people. The barracks were extremely overcrowded; people were sleeping in bunk beds three high. It was not meant to hold as many people as they brought in. Near

Barracks at Flossenburg. Wikimedia Commons/US Army

the end, Hungarian Jews and Polish gentiles from the Warsaw ghetto also were housed there.

When Nate arrived with Leon, they and the others were lined up in the square of the camp. There they were selected for various jobs.

Nate worked in a factory for two German engineers who were trying to perfect an experimental method of replacing airplane parts without using rivets. Their goal was to speed up the replacement process.

"On one occasion, I was sent to get a part and a foreman grabbed me and gave me 25 lashes on my back with a wire rope. No questions asked. He didn't realize I was sent to get parts by an engineer in another part of the building. After the beating, I could not sit down, so I stood. Because I was crying, one of the German engineers asked me what happened. I told him, and he walked away slowly. I felt he was sorry I had been beaten for no reason."

Still, the Germans demanded perfection. They were worried about sabotage to their repaired planes by the Jewish workers. Nate remembers that if the rivets weren't 100 percent flush with the plane, he'd get a beating. Those who just arrived from Hungary or from the Warsaw ghetto didn't know what to do. Though Nate was young, he gave orders for the work. One man had to be on one side of the plane to hold the panel so Nate could pound the rivet flush.

One engineer was nice. Nate cleaned the office for him once a

The crematorium at Flossenburg. Wikimedia Commons/Concordiadomi

week and was allowed to pick up leftover food – scraps of bread, other things with real butter on them. By doing that, Nate had an extra piece of bread he could give his brother, who lived in the same barrack with him.

At Flossenburg, they had only the bare minimum to eat. People were dying from starvation, disease and illness. No doctors were available for treatment.

"On occasion, we were inspected for lice. Everyone had lice," he said. "When they took us to the showers, the cold water was turned on. If anyone tried to step out of the water, they were pushed back and beaten. The showers didn't destroy the lice because there was no soap. We slept on straw mattresses that were infested with lice and bugs.

"One time I remember there was a dead person lying in bed next to me," Nate said. "Some people lay dead for days before someone took them away. The one small crematorium couldn't handle the volume so outside the barracks you could see stacks of dead people. They were piled high on wood and then burned. I saw this everyday. It became routine."

Today Nate realizes he really couldn't comprehend the odor and the emotions because of his young age, and because of how the Nazis made them live. While in the camps, he didn't linger on details and had to accept it all as a fact of life.

"I remember, though I try to forget, that my friend next to me found a human finger in his soup. It didn't disturb me anymore.

Double fences at the Flossenburg camp.
www.holocaustresearchproject.org

I just kept eating. I didn't look. I just ate — that was the animal part that came in. I didn't think about anything, just survival. I adapted myself to being an animal. That became the routine."

At this time, he had no idea what had happened to his sisters or any family members. He wasn't sure who was left alive. There had never been any goodbyes.

In Flossenburg, to even think of escape was to invite certain death. There were electric fences and barbed wire. If people tried to escape, they were caught and shot.

"Once when those in the barracks didn't report an escape plan, they took 10 people and hung them in front of us," Nate said. "I still have a photo of this, given to me by one of the guards, but it's too awful to share. Many other things were going on then that either I don't remember or I just blocked out of my mind."

8

March To Nowhere

One day in March or April of 1945, when Nate was about 17, an announcement came over the Flossenburg loudspeaker telling all the Jews to gather in the middle of the camp. He remembers the non-Jews laughed and applauded, thinking the Jews would be killed.

Instead, they were loaded onto train cars — some open carriages, some not. They traveled for one or two days. The Jews knew the Americans were close: Planes circled, but only bombed train engines. They knew the cargo could be precious — people.

The American pilots were flying low and could see Nazi soldiers running away from the train to hide.

"The Americans accidentally shot one carriage," he said. "I remember a friend had a bullet go in his neck and then exit out his body. I never saw him again. This shooting continued for a few days. They replaced the locomotives and the planes came and shot again. We were making no headway, so they took us off the train and started us on a death march.

"I dragged my brother to the front with me," Nate said. "I knew if we were at the end that those who didn't keep up with the marchers would be shot. I assumed, by that time, he was ready to throw it in because of conditions we were under. He wanted to give up.

"Our destination was unknown. Day and night we walked. It was raining. We wore wooden shoes and had little food. The main idea was to stay in front. Those in back were weak and couldn't walk. We heard shooting, but I focused on keeping my strength so I wouldn't get shot.

In this historic photo, German citizens are made to witness the result of a Nazi death march. The bodies are of Jewish women who were killed or died during the march.
Wikimedia Commons/US Army

"We kept marching until finally they turned us into a forest and lined us up. There were maybe 40 to 50 left, and we'd started with hundreds. It looked like they were going to shoot us, but then a one-armed German Wehrmacht officer came and said the Americans were less than a kilometer away. He talked to the SS guards and suddenly they all disappeared.

"We all stood there in awe for a short time, then my brother and I and two others plus one Russian prisoner took off for a house in the distance. There were pigs on the outside and a trough of food. We attacked the food. A German farm lady saw us and was scared, but knew we were starved. She threw bread at us and went in."

They went into an old barn and hid in the hay. The Russian ate old rotten eggs and had horrible cramps. The rest of them didn't know what to do. Finally, Nate and Leon walked to a nearby town — Stumsreid — thinking they'd run into Americans there.

Indeed, they were greeted by American soldiers from the Third Army, who gave them food.

Shortly after liberation, Nate, 17½, wears pants given to him by liberating soldiers.

"I remember a large can of jam. A Jewish soldier tried to take it away because he was afraid I'd get sick. They also gave us other food. We were among the first survivors these American soldiers encountered as they were heading toward the Czech border.

"They gave me a pair of pants that were so big they came up to my chest. I still have the photo," he said. "But I was happy not to have a camp uniform on. We found other survivors in an empty house. They'd found chickens and butchered them and were trying to make soup. The house owner found an American officer who spoke German and he made us leave.

"It created fear that even the Americans have Nazis. We ran away. Finally we found an American officer who spoke Yiddish. He found a place for us to stay in town. We stayed for five days. There was a big pot outside for cooking. The biggest thing was to eat. I developed a pot belly. At 17½, I was undernourished and afraid to stop eating. I was yearning for food."

9

Freedom And Resentment

A few days later, the men moved on and found the next city, Schwandorf, and other survivors. There the United Nations Relief Administration provided a large guest house with bunk beds, food and some clothing.

These photos are taken after liberation at the Schwandorf refugee camp. One shows Nate with his brother, Leon's wife Ruth and her mother.

While in Schwandorf, Nate took classes in making the upper part of shoes. The classes were sponsored by ORT, a worldwide Jewish charity.

While he was in Schwandorf, an American Army officer named Rothschild asked people if they could identify guards from Flossenburg and the death march. Nate and others were taken to Dachau, where SS soldiers were housed.

"I identified two of them and also had artifacts, including a photo of the Flossenburg hangings," he said. "Guards were sentenced to prison time by the American tribunal, but the time was very minimal. I believe they were soon released. I think they got away too easily.

"Rothschild was Jewish. He tried to get some punishment meted out. At this time, you could accept anything. Nobody gave a damn about the Jews then and before. To this day, I see Germans in their 80s and I suspect they might have been involved in killing my family."

Shortly after he arrived in Schwandorf, Nate remembers seeing an American Jewish entertainer, sponsored by the Joint Distribution Committee, who came to entertain the survivors.

"I was very resentful of the entertainer," Nate said. "He was constantly saying that he was telling his American family he was here to entertain. He was more like a commercial than a gesture of comfort."

This was an indication of Nate's building resentment toward the American Jewish community and its inaction during the war.

"In *May*, they sent us *winter* clothing — gloves, long underwear,"

These photos show Jewish refugees, including Leon (in top photo he's leaning over on the left side) and Nate (in bottom photo he's on the left with the group), at a memorial they made commemorating those who died on a Nazi death march from Flossenburg.

he said. "I started to resent the American Jewish attitude toward survivors because they were not really showing much care toward us, and they didn't help us at all."

Nate remained in Schwandorf for about 2½ years. While they were in Schwandorf, the remaining survivors made and dedicated stone memorials at several places along the road in memory of

Leon with his son Allen in Schwandorf.

those who died in the march. A rabbi conducted the memorial service and the group said the *Kaddish* prayer for the dead.

While in Schwandorf, Nate realized he'd had very minimal education and had no profession to depend on. He knew he needed to learn a trade.

Through vocational classes sponsored in Displaced Persons camps by the worldwide Jewish organization ORT, he completed a short course to learn to be an iron molder. Then he took another ORT class. This time he learned to make the upper part of shoes.

For a while, he and his brother Leon lived together. Then Leon met a survivor named Ruth in a different town and they married. Their son, Allen, was born the year Israel won its independence.

While they were in Schwandorf, Nate remembers being glued to the radio listening to news of Israel. Finally, on Nov. 29, 1947, they heard the famous partition vote that established Israel as a separate Jewish state. After Israel was declared a Jewish nation, survivors began heading there from Europe. Nate remembers reading letters from one survivor who talked about being held in Cyprus before the Haganah smuggled him and others into Israel. They also heard talk of others dying in the fight against the Arabs.

At this time, other survivors were headed to America, where they were sponsored by American relatives. With his new professional skills under his belt, Nate decided it was time to leave Germany, too.

He did not head to Israel or to the U.S.

"I did not feel I had to go to Israel and fight for some cause. I didn't have a reason — I'd lost everything," he said. "I felt it was the duty of the American Jews to fight for the State of Israel. I'd suffered enough."

Around this time, Leon felt compelled to go back to his hometown to search for family. He found no one. The Polish people there scared him purposefully because they feared he would want the family property back.

When Leon told Nate there were no survivors, Nate laid in bed dreaming, hoping and yearning that he could find a way to get his revenge against the Nazis.

"I was hoping that somehow, somewhere I would be drafted and have the opportunity to kill some Nazis for what they did to my family," Nate said. "It was a very strong feeling. I lost many nights thinking that I could join somewhere and find the SS and Gestapo that killed my family. It was especially strong because we found no survivors."

At that time, it was difficult for anyone to understand why people would try to eliminate an entire religious group.

"I understand it now," Nate said. "It wasn't just Poland: the killings occurred with the blessings of European countries. Not all, but many applauded the killing of Jews because of their upbringing in the church, where anti-Semitism was one of its biggest preachings."

After a while, Nate realized he was consumed by hate, and it was an emotion that was overpowering him. It boiled over when he saw an older German in Schwandorf. Nate thought he was one of the killers. "Maybe rightly so," he said, "because it took an awful lot of people to kill six million.

"Then I realized if I keep on living with hate it will destroy my mind because hate doesn't accomplish anything. But I promised myself I'll never forget, nor forgive, those people until the end of my life."

10

A New Country, A New Home, New Troubles

"I wanted to get as far away from Europe as I could get," Nate recalled.

He briefly considered going to Argentina, where his oldest brother, Jochinam (now Juan), had moved in 1928, when Nate was only an infant. But Nate didn't know where his brother was and he had no sponsorship to that country.

Then he saw an advertisement from the Australian government saying that it would accept a small percentage of Jews into the country.

Before he was allowed to go, he submitted to interviews and medical and psychological tests to ensure that he was healthy. He went with 10 other survivors — four women and six men.

To learn more about his new country and to satisfy a hunger for knowledge, Nate became an avid newspaper reader while awaiting transport to Australia. He also got maps of the world and studied geography — anything that would be beneficial to his

Oldest brother, Jochanim, in Argentina (1930)

Nate worked for the Australian Army after coming to that country.

education.

For the first leg of his trip in 1948, he was put on a train headed to Genoa, Italy. From there he boarded a ship called the *Castle Bianca* (White Castle) and was en route for 30 days.

While on board, he learned that most of the 900 non-Jewish immigrants were from Lithuania, Latvia, Estonia or the Ukraine and that they had participated in war-time atrocities toward Jews.

"As far as I was concerned, they participated with the SS and they were received by the Australians without being subjected to quotas or restrictions," Nate said, still frustrated by the circumstance even after all these years.

The Australian government paid for transportation, and gave them clothing and a small amount of money — all in exchange for a two-year contract to do paid work for the government.

Nate and three other Jewish survivors worked for the Australian Army at a camp near Sydney and Liverpool. He chose this option because it would take him away from the non-Jewish immigrants and also afford him opportunities to learn English.

Still, in the army kitchen, he and another survivor wound up working with some Latvians, who had tattoos under their arms signifying that they worked for the SS.

Around this time, the Sydney Jewish newspaper interviewed

Nate and his friend. The story was headlined: "Jewish survivors working amongst ex-Nazi collaborators." It was very obvious that the Australian government knew about those people, and it was ignored.

"There was nothing we could do," Nate said simply. He worked in that kitchen for a year.

During this time, he made friends with an Australian soldier, somehow finding a way to communicate.

"He persuaded me to give him my concentration camp uniform and other artifacts so I would not have to live with that horror any more. It was a kindness," Nate said.

While he was working with the army, Nate met a doctor who was the president of the Polish Jewish Association in Sydney. He tried to get acquainted with the Jewish community through him.

Through the Polish Jewish Association, Nate and the other Jewish survivors were assigned to Jewish families for the High Holidays.

"It was very dramatic, celebrating my first holidays after the war," Nate said. "I was 22 and I felt like a beggar. It reminded me of when I was young and my family brought in someone poor for the holidays. I had to leave after one day."

At another time, Nate was invited to the house of a family who had moved to Australia before the war. They asked him about his life experiences.

"When I told them we were full of lice and filthy, they asked if we took showers," he said. "I told them only with cold water in the dead of winter. One man, a German Jew, asked randomly, 'What brand of soap did you use?' The ignorant question stopped the conversation cold.

"I decided right then I'd never talk about my life experiences. I took it with a grain of salt, like it didn't happen and was not a concern. And I didn't speak about it for a long time."

After his year in the army, Nate was transferred to work with the Australian railroad. His job was to clean carriages, and he was happy to work there.

Though he attended an English class for a while, he mostly picked up the language on his own. The opportunity to learn English was the lure of this new job, especially because no other

For a while, Nate got involved in a restaurant partnership in Australia. Things fell apart when he was not named the chef.

foreign workers were employed there.

"I developed a good rapport with the Australian workers and they accepted me as one of them," Nate said. "It made me feel good."

Then reality set in. He was bored. He was far from his two brothers, who were both having problems of their own. He had no education, no bright future ahead. Nothing.

"At times, suicide became an alternative," Nate said. "Who would want to associate with a man with no education, no future, no money, nothing? Luckily, I decided suicide was too permanent and not a solution."

After his two years of service to the Australian government, Nate sought jobs through an employment office. The skills he'd learned from his ORT classes — iron molding and shoe-making — were obsolete.

But he did find work as a chef at Christian Brothers College. They gave him room and board and he cooked for the college students and 30 brothers and teachers. He kept that job for nearly two years.

After this job, he got involved in a restaurant partnership with a Hungarian Jewish man, but the deal soured when Nate was not designated as the chef. Lawyers had to get involved to untangle the mess.

At this time, Nate was staying in a rented room with a Jewish family from Warsaw. With borrowed money from the family, he became a salesman, selling ladies' clothing and menswear as well as towels and sheets. He often traveled to cities out in the country.

"I did this for about five or six years," Nate said. "I liked being on the road and amongst the Australians. I became a 'New Australian' and even picked up an accent.

"I was very proud of being an Australian citizen, a British subject. I had strong resentment toward Poland and its anti-Semitism. I found, after some years, that many New Australians were not nice to the Australians, and that bothered me. As a whole, I found them very accommodating."

Photos of Nate in Sydney, Australia, where he lived in the early 1950s.

11

Home To America

While in Australia, Nate kept in touch with Leon in Germany, and then in St. Louis after he and his family moved to the U.S. There Leon found their oldest brother-in-law, Mendel Schweber, who had been in the family for as long as Nate could remember, and maybe even before that.

Nate wrote to him. From Mendel's return letters, he learned that his sister and nephew had perished, and that his parents had been shot in the Tarnow ghetto. He also obtained his brother Juan's (Jochinam) address in Argentina. Nate wrote to him and got a letter back in Polish.

Juan and his family in Argentina. Nate reconnected with his eldest brother and helped him throughout his life.

Mendel also wrote to say Juan was destitute in Argentina.

"I decided to help him by sending a few pounds every time I wrote, even though I only earned 7 pounds every two weeks," said Nate, who continued to help his brother until his death at age 92 in 2004.

Nate also wrote to Leon and received letters back for a

period of time, then Leon stopped communicating.

"While I was in Australia, I received a letter from Leon, who was now living in Racine, Wisconsin. Leon wrote that he was ill and his wife was divorcing him. She was waiting for the day when we would be reunited so she could take their son and leave for another city."

In 1950, Nate applied for a visa to the U.S. In 1951, at the breakout of the Korean War, Nate received a letter from the consul to come for an interview. He met with a psychiatrist, a medical doctor and others, but even though he was an Australian citizen, the U.S. only recognized the country of origin. Because of a Polish quota, his visa wasn't approved until 1957.

He boarded a Pan Am flight for his first plane ride and flew to Fiji, then the Coral Islands. When the plane started overheating, they returned to the Coral Islands for repairs. After a three-day "vacation" in Hawaii, Nate made it to Los Angeles, then Chicago, where Leon and Ruth picked him up from the airport.

"Leon was in poor health. He had been hospitalized many times, and it was very depressing to me," Nate said. "Leon was depressed, and I was worried."

Leon had a secondhand store in Racine, where Nate worked for a short while before the brothers moved to Milwaukee. Nate had heard there were some Jews he knew in Germany who lived there. Nate rented a room from a Jewish family and started settling in and meeting other immigrants.

Among those he met were some Jewish men who were in the cattle business.

"I didn't know what to do and I figured with my meager education, I'd be suitable for this business, so I did it," Nate said of a profession he continued even after he turned 80.

His father, Avram Chaim, had been very knowledgeable about farming and animals. Nate remembers different farmers who would request his help with sick animals.

"Maybe it was meant for me to be in the cattle business," Nate said. "I do like animals. Maybe somehow I was driven to do that.

"At that time, I knew it was too late for education and I regret constantly that my educational opportunity had been taken from me and that I was not educated the way I'd like to be. The opportunity for schooling was not available because my business required me to get up at 4 a.m. and I was too tired to go to classes at night. But I became good and knowledgeable about what I was doing.

"I also did plumbing, repaired hair dryers — whatever needed doing. All my ventures were self-taught," Nate said.

12

The Love Of Family Again

In 1958, just as he was working to establish himself, Nate met Muriel Guten of Milwaukee, the woman he would marry. They were introduced by her uncle, Max Schumacher, who traveled in *greeneh* (immigrant) circles. They went on a triple date with two other couples, including Muriel's older brother, Donald, and his wife, Mimi. Nate endeared himself by bringing Muriel chocolate-covered cherries and flowers. Later, he scored even more points by fixing the brakes on her car.

"I was working in Kenosha and he was 'an engineer measuring the streets,'" Muriel joked. "I took him to my grandfather's deli, the family proving ground. My Grandpa Aaron used to sit on a stool and hold court. I introduced him to Nate and, as a sign of approval, he asked Nate if he wanted a corned beef sandwich."

They met in April and fell in love quickly. Muriel remembers

Nate with his children: daughter-in-law Nadia and sons Lonn and Craig, daughter Mindy.

how she, her sister, Renee, and sister-in-law, Mimi, watched through the window of her parents' house as Nate asked her father, Henry, for permission to marry her.

They were married Sept. 28, 1958.

"I had family again, and I was very well accepted," he said. "I was very much embraced by her family, and I felt I was really liked by them, even after a short time. We met in April, and got married in September. During that period, I created a close relationship with her uncles.

"I had the opportunity to marry survivors in Australia," he said of life before Muriel, "but I did not feel that I could withstand the constant reminder of the atrocities."

Craig, the first of three children, arrived in 1960. He was followed by Lonn and daughter, Mindy. Craig's Hebrew name is Avraham Chaim after Nate's father. Lonn's Hebrew name is Lazar after Nate's maternal grandfather. Mindy is named after Mindel, Nate's mother.

As his children grew, Nate placed much emphasis on their education. He promised them he would do everything to make sure they would get all the education they wanted — mostly because he yearned for it so much himself.

"All my children graduated from college, and I am very proud of them," Nate said.

In America, even with his wife and family, Nate didn't speak about his Holocaust experiences for a long time. Even so, those experiences very much shaped the man, husband and father Nate was becoming. His devotion and dedication to his wife and children is a living memorial to the family he lost during the Holocaust. Still, for the most part, his pain and memories were suffered in silence.

Leon fixes Nate's tie just before his wedding to Muriel.

"During the course of my life, if people asked about my history, I'd shake it off with comments like 'the KL tattoo on my arm went with my name before I changed it,'" Nate said. "Some of the farmers I worked with were curious, but I wouldn't go into deep conversation. It was too painful and I didn't want to open the wounds.

"My family and my three children didn't know the details of my personal experience, even though on many occasions they wanted to hear about it. I was afraid of how it would affect them. It's different when it's happened to your own family member. As they were growing up, I never discussed it. They knew I had been in a camp and lost my family."

Muriel said, "Obviously, he didn't want to talk about it. He never talked about it to the kids. I knew the general outline, and I think the kids just picked up bits and pieces."

Nate said, "I felt I was strong enough to keep it inside and live with it without going and opening wounds."

He also avoided being around other survivors because he did not want to be reminded of the past.

"Most survivors were scared enough and still lived in the past. When I came here I tried to associate with those who had no association with the Holocaust. It would have been devastating to me."

13

Reconnecting

On Nate's 60th birthday, his son Craig surprised him with a trip to Argentina to be reunited with his eldest brother, Jochinam (Juan), and his family in Buenos Aires. Craig had tracked down Alberto Taffel, Juan's son. Craig told him that his father, Nate, was Juan's youngest brother.

Nate didn't remember ever meeting Jochinam. Years before the war, when Nate was an infant, Jochinam wanted to leave Poland. His mother visited a rabbi for advice on where he should go. The rabbi retired to his room for more than an hour, then returned to tell her he should go to Argentina. So that's where he went.

Nate, Muriel and Craig made the journey together, and Nate met his brother for the first time with mixed emotions.

"I didn't know what to say, so I said, 'Our mother in heaven is looking at us. She's happy we are together.' Then we embraced," Nate said.

Juan gave Nate a family photo and also one of their youngest sister, Faiga. Juan received this picture from a survivor who had been with his sisters on a transport train. The woman, who moved to Argentina because she had family there, told Juan his sisters all drowned in a river in Poland en route to Treblinka, sentenced to that watery death because Auschwitz was at full capacity. The woman had seen a document with the photo on it floating in the water and saved it to pass it on.

The Argentinian Taffel family was very poor. Juan had three daughters and a son, but one of his daughters had died in a train accident. During their visit, the brothers spoke Yiddish, then one translated for his family into English, the other into Spanish.

Nate's youngest sister, Faiga, drowned in a river in Poland en route to Treblinka. A survivor found this photo floating on the water and passed it on to Juan when she met him in Argentina, where she settled.

"I visited him and his family five times," Nate said. "My whole family met them. On the last visit, when Juan was in his 80s, he told me his biggest desire was to go to Israel where his daughter had moved. He wanted to die in Israel. I arranged for him to move to Israel, and he lived with his daughter until he died at age 92."

The Taffels visited Israel five times and keep in touch with his niece and her family. In the summers of 2007 and 2009, he and Muriel were able to visit with his great-great-niece, Anat, from Migdal HaEmek (in Israel's Central Galilee region) when she attended a special program at Tamarack Camps near Detroit, Mich.

"I enjoy all kinds of happy events in the family and out of the family," Nate said. "Muriel and I very seldom miss any happy occasion, even if we have to travel long distances, but I do not like to attend funerals because I find that life is so beautiful and death is so permanent."

14

Living The Aftermath

For Nate, the effects of the Holocaust seeped into every seam of his life. Because he was so young when the war started (and only a teenager when he was in the camps), his physical development was delayed.

He says he didn't shave until he was 20. He didn't have pubic hair or sexual desires until he was 18½.

"I was very ignorant," he said. "I heard talk about sex, but I didn't know anything."

His self-confidence was damaged, too. This was a major stumbling block in his younger life, and one that lingers even now as a senior citizen. He is embarrassed by his lack of education, and admits to being emotional, especially when confronted by anything related to the Holocaust.

His brother, Leon, who had been selected among other young Jewish men to bury the Jews shot by the Nazis, suffered tremendous emotional trauma after the war. He felt horrific guilt for his role and thought people were accusing him of collaborating with the Nazis. He was in and out of mental institutions. He was especially tormented before he died in 1968.

Nate believes that all survivors suffered emotional damage. He says that even German psychiatrists admitted in 1949 that survivors had been damaged emotionally and psychologically at least 25 percent, with many sustaining more damage than that.

Nate learned that minimal contact with other survivors worked best for him.

"When I first came to America, I associated with other survivors for a short time, but it became depressing. No matter what, talk wound up being about the Holocaust and the atrocities. I couldn't stand it."

Nate is known among friends and family as a jokester with a good sense of humor, sometimes a little corny but always entertaining. His bright blue eyes light up when he's in the midst of a joke.

"My sense of humor helped me survive," he said seriously. "If not for my sense of humor, I wouldn't be talking to you today. I did not allow myself to go into depression after many years. I don't enjoy depressing things.

"I understand you can't avoid sad things in life, no matter how you try to avoid them. To lighten things up, you use your sense of humor."

He still steers clear of blatant reminders of the horrors he witnessed firsthand. He never watches Holocaust-related movies, for example.

"On a trip to Israel, I walked two feet into Yad Vashem and saw the photos of the young Jewish kids and it broke me up. I couldn't proceed," he said. "I don't watch Holocaust movies or go to any Holocaust museums, though I am a charter member of the U.S. Holocaust Museum and my family's names are inscribed at the Miami Holocaust Center and at Yad Vashem in Israel, and at Temple Beth Israel in Milwaukee."

By 1994, Nate was ready to show his grown children his roots. They went to Germany, rented a car and went to Flossenburg to see the labor camp where Nate had worked.

"In town, we asked where the camp was, and we were told there was no such thing by the residents," Nate said. "Knowing I had been there, someone eventually told us about it."

At the site, all the barracks were destroyed as well as the burial ground in the middle of the camp. There were concrete walls listing how many people from each country were killed there. A standing building served as a memorial to those who were killed.

"Very little was left," Nate said. "It looked like a park. I had mixed feelings. I couldn't wait to get there — and to get out of there."

The family followed the route of the death march Nate had endured. The memorials they erected no longer were there. On

Nate's family home as it looks today on the square in Radomsyl Wielki.

the way to Schwandorf, they met a young German who remembered people from the concentration camp who had stayed with his grandfather, and he showed the area to them.

In Schwandorf, there were few reminders. The displaced persons camp was now a big store, and nothing resembled the days from the war. They then traveled to Poland to Warsaw, Krakow and Auschwitz. In Tarnow, Nate had no recollection of where the ghetto had been.

"It was hard for me everywhere we went," Nate said. "I often waited outside for my family. It was too difficult and emotional to re-open the wounds."

This trip marked the first time he had been back in his hometown of Radomysl Wielki. He went to city hall and wanted to find documents of the Taffels, but was told all Jewish records had been destroyed by the Germans.

On the square, he found four older Polish women and started talking to them in Polish. He found out one remembered his sister, and all remembered the house, which was right down the block. He talked to them for quite a while. The women were crying.

Nate had always told his family his house was the largest in the city, and when they found it, they saw it was.

"I went to my house, and a retired gentile principal approached me and opened the door to the house," Nate said. "It had been re-done, with electricity and indoor plumbing added. In one

On his second trip back to Poland, Nate and family members attended the dedication of a memorial to the Jews of Radomsyl. With him is Jan Gibron, the school principal who kept a memorial museum in the building where Nate's family lived.

apartment, the man was very proud to show a collection of Jewish artifacts he had turned into a museum. I was impressed.

"I had received information from others about how non-Jews had reacted after the Jewish people were liquidated from the city. They fought over Jewish properties like vultures," he said.

Nate walked into his old house and says he felt bittersweet.

"I felt a tremendous sadness when I saw the rooms that were there without my family. I fought my emotions, but I wanted to leave and get away from the memories. I didn't want to upset my family," he said.

Muriel says Nate didn't start talking about his story until they got to Radomysl.

In Mielec, he wanted to visit the place where he had worked in the airplane factory.

"I went into one place, but my emotions couldn't take it any more and I said, 'Let's get out of here,'" Nate recalled. They went back to Warsaw, then Berlin. The children returned home, while Muriel and Nate went on to Israel.

"I was overloaded with emotions," Nate said. "On that trip, I told my family the largest part of my experience. I wanted to go on that journey, but it was hard."

On his second trip to Europe, this time with his wife, son Craig, sister-in-law Miriam Guten of Dallas, her sister Charlotte Strauss of Los Angeles and their cousin Bobbie Shafton of Milwaukee, Nate attended a Holocaust dedication in Radomysl Wielki. They also visited sites of the former Prague ghetto and ghettoes in various countries.

During the ceremony in Radomysl, a stone was unveiled in the cemetery by Jan Gibron, the Polish school principal who is still gathering Jewish artifacts. Jews who came to the dedication from France, Israel and the United States said the *Kaddish* (mourner's prayer) together.

"People don't realize how blessed they are to be able to see where their loved ones are buried and they can see a gravestone," Nate said. "I had no opportunity to see where my parents died. I wish they had died a normal death and had been buried with dignity and with a gravestone. I have no idea when or where or how they died.

"I constantly think how traumatic it must have been for such wonderful parents to have been shot by a bullet or gassed. It has stayed with me since I found out about the elimination of my family. How horrific it had to have been for them, knowing their destiny. It's constantly in my mind. Even though now I talk about it, I still feel very emotional. No one else can feel the same way except a survivor who lost his family under such tragic events."

Nate was surprised on this trip to discover quite a few Jewish people moving back to the European countries where they still weren't wanted.

"Anti-Semitism still exists there," Nate said. "I do not want to go back. I have been living in this country for 50 years and there's no other country I'd like to live in. I got so Americanized. When I became a citizen, I became more idealistic."

15

Reawakening Heart

With all he'd experienced and lost during the Holocaust, Nate found he had much hatred in his soul toward the German people. He still tries to avoid anything produced in Germany.

"I was very disturbed by the fact that millions of Jews were killed. Because they were displaced people, the country of origin didn't return property to the rightful owners and heirs, and the world remains silent," he said.

"I would like to get my property back — the house and farmland — not for the material value, but because the house belongs to me. I wasn't a traitor. I didn't leave my country on my own free will. Why am I deprived of my property and need permission to walk into my own house? The world is waiting for the survivors to die out and forget about the history and their property.

"To this day, I cannot understand why the world does not make countries, especially Poland, which had millions of Jewish people, give back Jewish property. Now they are a democracy and not communist. As you can tell, I resent how the Polish people acted toward the Jews. I do want to emphasize there was a small percentage of Polish people who hid Jews, and for that some lost their lives. Unfortunately, Jews had no way of escaping because they were hated by most of the people. I would like to know what excuse they have for not returning our property?

"After all the anti-Semitic things the Poles did to the Jewish people, you would think, after the war, that they would be compassionate enough to say to the Jewish people, 'No more anti-

Semitism, and the properties you left behind, we either compensate you or you can move back into your places.'

"My theory is, after reading and knowing Hitler's ideas of eliminating the Jewish people, that Poland welcomed it because Hitler would deal with a population they never wanted. Also, there must have been a fear by the anti-Semites that the way the Jewish population was increasing they would be overrun in so many years. The idea of Hitler eliminating the Jewish people would have suited them very well. I'm also not a bit surprised that all the gas chambers, all the death camps that existed were on Polish land.

"Maybe in years to come — I won't be able to know — but some people might find some documents showing that Poland was very excited about Hitler's ideas. As it is right now, history wouldn't come out with any of the information, if it exists.

"It amazes me that it took approximately 60 years to open the files kept by the Germans listing all the people they killed. Only now, as the last of the Holocaust survivors are dying, they finally come out with it. I still haven't gotten the opportunity to find out what happened to my family, and I was a teen. Most of the survivors are old and feeble. Once they are gone, who will care?

"To this day, I also can't understand why the Americans and English didn't bomb the barracks of the SS or the killing facilities. Even though there would have been casualties among the Jews, they might not have had to go to the gas chambers like sheep," Nate said.

"Future generations will wonder why we didn't fight back. The Orthodox Jewish people believed the killers will be punished by God, and the young people willing to go fight didn't have any help from the non-Jewish population. For example, my cousins who were hiding in the forest had two kinds of enemies: the people who wanted to take their properties and the Nazis who wanted to kill them. In some cases, they were killed by Germans who were told where they were hiding. One of my cousins survived and he had to move from place to place until he found one gentile man who helped him and provided him with some food he could pick up during the night."

After liberation, these thoughts flooded Nate's mind, and the hatred grew.

"Finally, I decided that if I live with this animosity, it will destroy me," Nate said. "I can't live with hate. I finally got my normal senses back. I decided there's no sense in me hating, except that I would destroy myself if I surrendered to the hate."

Now, after these long years of silence, when Nate brings his story to school groups and other audiences, one of his most poignant messages is that hate destroys.

16

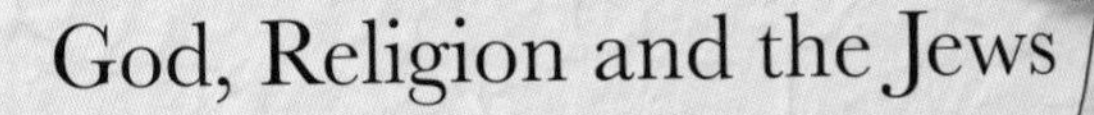

God, Religion and the Jews

Nate was born into an Orthodox Jewish family. The foundation was laid by his parents, who taught him from a young age to be a decent citizen. As he grew older, Nate's own feelings of spirituality evolved.

"I can pray to God wherever I am," he said. "To me, the universe is my temple. I believe in God more for fear of not believing. It's easy to accept God. Why take a chance and not?

"What I don't understand is how religious people of various faiths can go out and kill innocent people in the name of the Messiah. All religions preach to love your neighbor as yourself. How can the masses not question that? To me, it's hypocrisy."

Though he came from an Orthodox family that observed all the laws of *kashruth* (keeping kosher) and where every holiday was celebrated, Nate became a Reform Jew. He and Muriel raised their children in this environment at Temple Emanu-El B'ne Jeshurun in Milwaukee. Nate used the opportunity to learn more about the Jewish religion, and to give his children a religious education so they could decide for themselves.

He and his family celebrate the major Jewish holidays together and the experiences are bittersweet.

"I don't look forward to the High Holidays because it reminds me of my family," he said. "Passover is the worst because in our home in Poland it was a tremendously joyous family gathering, with all the family together.

"As a child, I remember we all went to the baker who had to make sure there wasn't any flour or chametz for Passover. We would bring our own flour and ingredients to make sure everything was kosher for Passover. We rolled the dough and made the matzahs. My job was putting in the holes. We would sing together with lots of happiness.

"Our house was free of chametz, and our Passover dishes were brought out. My mother and sisters prepared the food together, and they enjoyed themselves. Being the youngest, I had to ask the Four Questions. But it was very late, and I went to sleep. The celebration went late into the night.

"I was brought up in a family with dignity, passion, reality, forgiveness and charity in the sense of obeying the Torah," he says.

"It was not God's will to destroy people. The human race needs someone to kill or mistreat because of hunger for power and domination. People are always looking for scapegoats for our failures. The weak people of the world especially are targets – then and today. The Jews had no defense.

"The Holocaust could happen again. It could happen to anybody. History repeats itself. Anti-Semitism flourishes when a country is not doing well because they need someone to blame.

"Me — I have *yahrtzeit* every day," he said of the Jewish custom of remembering the anniversary of loved ones' deaths with prayer.

"It may sound silly, but I attribute my survival to my mother in heaven who protected me so there would be someone to say *Kaddish* for them. At least one person would be able to survive and tell the world, which I now feel obligated more than ever before to do. I don't use 'luck' in situations like this. It's destiny."

17

Deciding To Speak Out

Before Nate decided to speak publicly about his Holocaust experiences and the lessons he learned so cruelly, he recorded his life story in 2000 as part of the Steven Spielberg Film and Video Archive at the U.S. Holocaust Memorial Museum in Washington, D.C. He also did a taped interview with the Miami Institute for Jewish Learning. Both tapes are available to people requesting speakers.

"Spielberg sent out four people to my house and spent three to four hours talking to me and recording my experiences. That was really the first time I let myself be interviewed and it might not have been a full accounting because now, during the few years I've been speaking in public, I've let a lot of memories come back that for so many years I've tried to hide.

"The videos were very hard to do. The first time a lot of things came out that I had kept within. I did it mostly in memory of my family. They deserved it. I was the only survivor in the family to put everything together.

"I was asked to speak to colleges, high schools, different groups," Nate said. "I was contacted by the Coalition of Jewish Learning of the Milwaukee Jewish Federation after the videos, but it was very difficult, especially after opening the wounds, and I didn't realize I was capable of talking to the public about my experiences.

"I was afraid of what it would do to me mentally, but it was a process of looking at the pros and cons. The pros won. I felt my family would want me to do it. And, besides, not all things in life are easy. Every person knows how much his mentality can take

Nate speaks to many student groups and tells them of his Holocaust experiences. The importance of spreading his message outweighs the trepidation he feels about speaking and the emotions that are always just below the surface.

before being affected, and I hadn't lost my faculties yet and I was 75. I thought I should have enough strength to do this."

In about 2004, they called again.

"Sandy Hoffman of Milwaukee, one of the founders of the national organization Second Generation, wanted me to consider speaking because most of the survivors were getting to be very old and immobile, and passing away," Nate said. "Something came up in my mind to say right away that I will do it. I felt an obligation to do it for my family."

The first talk was to high school students; most were not Jewish. Nate remembers having a sleepless night the night before. He had never spoken publicly before. He was nervous because he didn't know how the students would react.

"I was worried about how speaking out about my experiences would affect me, if it would give me sleepless nights and flashbacks and open all the atrocities that happened to me and my family again. I didn't know if I was ready for that."

That morning he was excited and trying to recall all the things that had happened to him and his family. He did not — and still does not — speak from notes or a script. It all comes from the heart. He says it hasn't gotten easier to speak publicly about his experiences, but he knows he must do it.

"Since that first time, I've talked to thousands of kids and adults — mostly non-Jewish at parochial schools," Nate said. "As long as I'm able, I'll continue because of the difference I'm making in people's lives. Letters come in the mail from people moved by my story, and that outweighs my emotions and trepidations.

"I've read some of the letters three or four times, and some make me cry. They tell me how much I have changed their lives. I am very cognizant of the fact that I could bore them. But when 300 kids don't cough or move, it means something. They come up and hug me, and I have a tendency to break down."

During his speeches, which have been given at colleges, high schools, middle schools, churches and synagogues, he emphasizes the self-destructive nature of hate. It's the most powerful part of his speech, even though other parts of his story often reduce audience members, even men, to tears.

That denunciation of hate is a prime motivation for his speeches, which always are painful, draining and emotional. Yet he wants his message to be heard loud and clear.

"I emphasize to the kids that if someone tells you to hate, you must question why," Nate says. "If you give in to the hate, you'll destroy yourself. Hate doesn't help anything. If you believe in God and the hereafter, you know those who hate and who participated in killing innocent people will have to face the consequences. If they ever dreamed of getting into Heaven, they will be very disappointed."

He says he gets choked up and often cries while he's giving a speech. Taking a mild tranquilizer beforehand helps sometimes. And he says he's not always sure where his speech will take him. Occasionally, memories he's forgotten or buried surface to surprise him. Each memory adds to the power of his story.

Is talking about his Holocaust experience good therapy?

"If it isn't, I have to sacrifice," he said. "If it hurts, I can't help it. I've got to do it."

Afterwards, he says, students have come up to him to tell him they've seen several Holocaust movies, but that listening to him has really made them think.

"My talk has a tremendous persuasion on them," Nate said, not bragging about his public speaking abiltities but confident about his ability to deliver a life-altering message.

He also emphasizes that the most important thing in people's lives is family. The second most important is teachers.

"Without them, where would we be?" he asked. "I, without any formal education, can tell you how much I missed that. It certainly would have made my life much easier. Unfortunately, I missed both an education and the joy of a life that included my family."

Nate also shares rare existing photos of his family he got from his brother in Argentina, of the memorials to those on the death march and also photos of himself in Australia. He also shows examples of valueless money made by prisoners in Flossenburg. This was given to political prisoners and homosexuals to use. Many listeners want to see his "KL" tattoo.

At his talks, there's always time for questions. People mostly ask about religion, politics and his family. He's even had some students come to his house to talk with him more about religion and the belief in God, especially after the horrors of the Holocaust.

He's often asked if the Holocaust could happen again.

"It could happen to anybody," he said. "History repeats itself. It's happening in Darfur and other places and, unfortunately, we don't do much about it. I imagine any country with any economic or political problems looks for scapegoats and will pick a minority.

"Some leaders of the world like to conquer other countries.

Nate with his daughter Mindy, who is named after his mother, Mindel. She says she learns more details of his story every time she hears him speak to a group.

By doing that, they kill people for no reason except to show their superiority or dominance. For instance, Saddam Hussein, who tried to conquer Kuwait and Iran, where he killed an enormous amount of people inside and outside of his country. If we wouldn't have stopped him, he would have destroyed many more thousands of lives.

"If we don't continue to stop the leaders seeking more power and destruction of human beings with nuclear weapons or other means, the world will not get better; it will get worse. And still, one way or another, we'll have a holocaust. If we'd stopped Hitler from conquering Czechoslovakia and Austria, we maybe would have avoided a second world war."

Recently, he's spoken to bigger groups, sometimes up to 400 people. In 2009, he had two important speaking engagements during Yom HaShoah (Holocaust Remembrance Day), a day in April designated around the world to remember those who died in the Holocaust as well as those who survived. Nate spoke at Milwaukee's community program, and his son, Lonn, arranged for him to speak at his synagogue in Northbrook, Ill. At this event, sister-in-law Mimi Guten came up from Dallas to hear him for the first time. Lonn, his wife, Nadia, and their son, Noah, also attended as well as Nate's other children, Mindy and Craig. Muriel always accompanies Nate when he speaks to groups.

"Watching him speak with such heartfelt emotion about his early years is very difficult for me," Mindy said. "Each time I hear him tell his story I continue to learn more details. To hear him share his experiences with a group of strangers confirms what a strong man he is. I'm proud he has found the strength to deliver such an important story."

"Throughout the years, there was minimal talk about his early life," Mindy said. "I just got bits and pieces. It wasn't until we took the trip to Poland and Germany in 1992, and we saw where he lived and what he went through in the concentration camps, that he started talking about his life.

"The most rewarding part about his speaking is when he gets the letters from those who have heard his story. He reads each and every one. I'm so proud of him for enduring the pain and passing on his experiences. It does not get easier for him each time he speaks, yet he does it."

18

Compassionate Adviser

Wise, compassionate and generous to family and friends, Nate also has a devilish streak that makes him a bit of a troublemaker. He teases good-naturedly and often commands the floor to tell dated, sometimes off-color jokes that he laughs at himself. Sometimes he sings out loud, often funny songs that make you smile. When he purses his lips, and double-blinks those bright blue eyes, watch out — something funny is coming. Or at least something *he* thinks is funny.

Like this one:

"There was the most righteous person on the Earth who gave *tzedakah*, or charity. He was very honest and spoke no evil and followed the Ten Commandments. Anyway, he dies. Well, he comes up to heaven and is greeted by Moses, who says, 'Oh, my son. I'm so glad you're here. I've been waiting for you all my life. Now that you're here, I'm going to make us some lunch.' So Moses goes into the kitchen and comes back with lunch, and the righteous person looks at the peanut butter and jelly sandwich. He looks, and in hell he sees they're eating steaks and the best food you can imagine. He turns around to Moses, 'What gives? Here you give me a peanut butter and jelly sandwich and there they're getting the best food you can imagine.' Moses tells him, 'Here it doesn't pay to cook for two.' The morale to the story: Not too many people make it to heaven."

Nate, of course, laughed at this.

"My sense of humor helped me survive," he said simply. "If not for my sense of humor, I wouldn't be here today. I did not allow myself to go into depression after those years. I don't enjoy depressing things.

"I understand you can't avoid sad things in life, no matter how hard you try. To lighten them up, I use my sense of humor."

But don't try to get him laughing during a card game or at the casino. There he's dead serious and very focused, even tense on occasion. It's just another side of Nate, one where he calls upon his intelligence and intellect to best an opponent.

But you could never have a better person on your side. When it comes to human relations, Nate is an expert, or a self-declared expert, especially when it involves family. These ties are sacred to Nate, who knows how devastating it can be to lose them — or to have them torn from you.

Feuding family members and friends stand no chance against his considerable powers of reconciliation.

"I had an instance in my family when one of my nephews married a non-Jewish girl and his mother called and asked if I'm coming to the wedding. My response was not only am I coming to the wedding, but I'm bringing the whole family. If they love each other, then religion does not become a factor. By us not going, we only hurt him, and I don't like to hurt part of my family."

Nate's response helped the parents, too.

"In business associations, on many occasions, I've been asked about marriage and bringing up children. Not that I'm the smartest person, but being a survivor of a large family, I'm very compassionate and cognizant of the fact that no matter what, you've got to reach out, and also that no one person is always right. It takes two people to create happiness and forgiveness."

He has stepped in on several occasions as a father figure for relatives who lost their own father much too early. He understands that void because he says it never leaves him. And he always lends an ear as a trusted adviser for family and friends with troubles. He finds ways to cut to the heart of what aches and to provide counsel and support. You may have to listen to a few bad jokes along the way, but it's worth it.

19

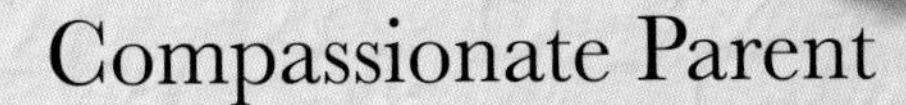

Compassionate Parent

Nate's Holocaust experiences had an influence on his parenting of his three children.

"On many occasions, I would tell my children that if I did something I was uncomfortable with, I would apologize and tell them I didn't have a role model to learn from because I lost him at such an early age. What I remember of my father was that he was subdued and quiet, honorable, very respectable. Very seldom did he get mad. He bought me four pigeons, a porcupine to play with, a dog. I was not deprived of too many things. He spoiled me."

Muriel says Nate is like his father in that he spoiled their children.

"He was not the disciplinarian," she said. "He would send a child who had to be disciplined to me, saying that I would spank them. One specific incident, when Mindy was born and I was in the hospital, Lonn had been caught lighting matches. He was 4 at the time. I asked the pediatrician what to do with him, and he said, 'Beat the shit out of him!' And the doctor didn't believe in hitting a child. It was that serious of an offense.

"Nate went home and Lonn was hiding in the closet. Far from beating the shit out of him, he told him that if he burned the house down, they'd have to live in the streets.

"Once he needed to discipline Craig, this was before the other children were born, and he felt so bad about it he went out and bought him toys," Muriel said. "I don't think he ever disciplined any of them again."

"I was over-protective of the kids because I adored them," Nate said. "I was constantly worried something could happen to them. We had a wired intercom, one of the first ones, and you could hear the kids cough."

He remembers searching the neighborhood for Lonn after he'd been missing for several hours. He'd been eating cookies next door. Several times he remembers calling the hospitals if kids came home late.

Still, Nate allowed his kids to participate in sports. All of them were involved.

"On many occasions, I was saddened because I didn't have a father to guide me and provide an example of how to raise a family," Nate said. "I have allowed my children to make their own decisions. The results have been tremendous. I have the best family I could possibly wish for.

"I must have done a good job of bringing up my children because I feel so much love that they give me, and I am always very proud of them," Nate said. "As youngsters in high school, they were always working and having good grades. If they had problems with teachers, I'd tell them I'd buy the school and put in teachers they liked. That would stop them from complaining.

"The kids always had a car when they were teens because they needed one to go to work. I trusted them with their behavior. Alcohol in my house was never locked up. I trusted them."

Mindy said, "He hated to see us struggle and would tell us not to take things so seriously. But he does, and I am similar in that way. He often would tell me, after what he's overcome in life, we can overcome anything. Sometimes when I sit back and put in perspective what he's overcome, any challenges I might be going through are a small bump in the road compared to what he's been through.

"He's always instilled that family is the most important thing to him. It brings him tremendous joy to have us around."

Nate said, "And I'm grateful for my son, Lonn, and daughter-in-law Nadia for giving me the most gorgeous, wonderful grandsons (Noah and Jonah) I could hope for. I can't wait to participate in at least one bar mitzvah." (Noah's is set for fall 2010.)

Nate and Muriel are the boys' true fans, traveling from Milwaukee to Chicago often to see their grandsons participate in

Nate, his son, Lonn, and his beloved grandsons, Noah and Jonah.

various sports.

"He's a remarkable man, my role model and hero; he's my father," Lonn said. "Deprived of his youth and formal schooling, that didn't prevent my father from becoming a successful businessman and, more importantly, husband and father. Strong as an ox, a harder-working man you'll never meet. Day in and day out, my father woke up at 4 a.m. to go to work. He did so to provide for what means most to him — his family.

"In good times and in bad," Lonn said, "I could always count on my father being there. For that I am so very thankful. Seldom does a day go by that I don't speak with my dad. To me, my dad's more than the father of the year, he's the father of a lifetime."

Regarding his experiences in the Holocaust, the kids knew he was a survivor, Muriel says, but no details, except that he had been in a concentration camp.

"They would ask, but I never went into details," Nate said. "It became more of an interest to them after I received the pictures of my family from my brother in Argentina. Then they asked about the family; still I didn't go into detail. They knew not to question me because they could see my expressions. I imagine they knew more than I could possibly realize because we have a tendency not to give the children as much credit as they deserve."

Nate kept most of his Holocaust story to himself. Even Muriel didn't know the whole story for many years.

"I knew enough, so I didn't want to push the subject," she said. "And then finally, in 1994, when we took the family to Europe, he started telling some of the story as we went to the different camps and cities where he'd been.

"I had been a history minor at the University of Wisconsin and had studied the Holocaust, so I had some idea. When he told me where he'd been, I had an idea of what happened there."

20

Sanctity Of Life

When Nate had a heart attack at age 54, he was very distressed because he had upset his family.

"I was sad for upsetting them," he recalled.

When it comes to health issues, Nate tends to look at the gloomy side.

"I always think tests will come back negative. Those are scars I obtained from the concentration camp. It had an effect on me.

"When I had the heart attack, I thought that was it," he said. "I was afraid I'd die at a young age and not see my family prosper and have their own families and grandchildren.

"I saw so many die at a young age that I had a tremendous fear of death. To me, death was scary. It always reminded me that when people die, it leaves a scar. For many years, I didn't like to go to cemeteries. I am a *kohan* (Hebrew for priest) and we are not supposed to go to cemeteries. I used that excuse for many years.

"Throughout the years in the livestock business, I had to take cattle to the slaughterhouse and see them being driven to slaughter. It was a constant reminder of how the Jewish people and my family had been treated the same way. I feel uncomfortable at the slaughterhouse and don't like the killings. I feel sorrow for the young animals. I feel regret. And I visualize how my family could've been executed. I rationalize that maybe the cattle don't know what's happening to them. They just go and don't fight — just as the Jewish people did even though they knew what was going to happen and had no choice. But that's how the Nazis treated people."

Despite these deep emotions, Nate thrived in the cattle business.

He got his first cattle truck in 1958.

Over the years, many of these farmers in rural Wisconsin became good friends, somewhat of an extended family, that put him in touch with his agrarian roots in Poland. Non-Jewish with large families, these farmers often invited Nate to breakfast or a meal, and he and Muriel shared joyous occasions with them and their families.

With most of the farmers, Nate didn't go into details about the Holocaust. They knew he went through concentration camps, but he tried to avoid the conversations.

"I wouldn't have a conversation with a customer for pity's sake," he said.

Since 2003, Nate has been in semi-retirement, only working one or two days a week. Now 82, Nate is on the verge of quitting altogether. He spends much of the winter in Florida to avoid the harsh Wisconsin winters. He only retains customers he has a close relationship with, and looks forward to visiting with them more than actually doing business. A handful of them have come to hear him speak publicly about the Holocaust.

"A lot of them could not believe the atrocities I went through," Nate said. Now they want to bring their whole families to listen to him when he speaks nearby.

21

Thoughts On Israel

Though Nate decided not to move to Israel after the war and went to Australia instead, he does have strong feelings for the Jewish state, which he has visited five times.

"Having a religious upbringing, being in Israel had an emotional effect on me. Seeing firsthand the sights I was taught about in Hebrew classes, I had a sense of belonging, and of safety.

"The Jews need Israel now more than ever," he said. "History has taught us that anti-Semitism doesn't go away. We were assured that after the atrocities of World War II, anti-Semitism would disappear and be replaced by more brotherly love. Unfortunately, that hasn't happened.

"Religious people constantly read 'Love Thy Neighbor,' and it's beautifully written, but unfortunately it's not executed in the world.

"I do blame most of the hate on various religions and people who interpret religion in their own way of thinking. If it ever happens that we should really love our neighbor regardless of religion, race or color, I would like to live that long and see it. I doubt it will happen because a scapegoat is still needed."

Nate is very outspoken about suicide bombers that have been plaguing Israel and its citizens for years.

"People of a sound mentality won't sacrifice their lives without thinking of why and what for," he said. "They are persuaded by another person who takes advantage of their mental problem. Any leader who tells people to kill for no reason — but doesn't want to do it himself — especially if they are very religious and observant, is no leader.

"If my rabbi would tell me to kill, I'd consider him not fit for religious leadership and I would participate in his ouster as a leader. I don't know of any Jewish leader who would go tell someone to blow himself up.

"We have to be strong for the sake of survival," Nate said. "History taught us that defenseless people get killed. We have to be strong to protect ourselves and not kill if there is no cause for it.

"I could not imagine after Hitler and the killings by his followers that, in this day and age, we would still have Neo-Nazis who believe in his theories. I get so upset when I read about them in the papers, that those kinds of imbeciles could follow a murderer.

"It still boils down to the silent majority that takes those people for granted and assumes they are irrelevant. That's what happened when Hitler came to power."

22

Touching Lives

Through his years of speaking about his experiences, Nate has been awarded many certificates of appreciation that hang on the wall of his den. He especially prizes the many letters he's received from middle school, high school and college students as well as teachers after his speeches.

He finds especially meaningful a banner given to him by students from a Germantown, Wisconsin school. The students left him messages and drew pictures thanking him for sharing his message.

Muriel and Nate stand before a mural made by middle-school students in appreciation to Nate for sharing his life story.

Muriel and Nate

"I feel rewarded and appreciated and proud that I am recognized," he said. "I feel, after I'm gone, there will still be documentation — tapes, videos, newspaper stories and this memoir — of what happened to me and my family and the Jewish people.

"If someone said the Holocaust didn't happen," Nate said, "I would put my life up against theirs and prove that it did. They are either publicity-seekers or anti-Semitic."

He has a special album that contains many of these original letters, including some handwritten by younger students. Each, in its own way, conveys how moved the individual was by Nate's life story and by his message not to hate. The empty pages of the album are filling up fast, and Nate, understanding the importance of speaking out, plans to continue his talks to groups as long as he can. He already has many speaking engagements booked into the future.

To him, it's all about "bearing witness and being a part of living history."

"The biggest reward in my speaking is the kids' appreciation toward telling my story," Nate said. "It's overwhelming to me — the hugs and kisses and the letters and donations on my behalf.

It makes the pain of speaking about my experiences worthwhile, especially when I run into young adults and teachers who recognize me and give me a hug and tell me I made a difference in their lives."

Letters

May 21st, 2007.

Dear Mr. Taffel,

I will start off by saying thank you so much for coming and sharing your story with us. You really touched me. I have learned that you should never take your family for granted, or even your life in general. It was honestly the best speech that I have ever heard. I could never do what you do. I'm to weak. To be a part of the Holocaust would traumatize me. I don't think I would ever be able to talk about it. You are such an inspiration, no matter what situation, you can survive. That is what I took out of the speech, along with a few other lessons.

Again, thank you so very much. Your visit was a very enjoyable experience. I will be sure to pass this story on through further generations.

Yours truely,
Emily

Dear Mr.Taffel,

First I would like to say wow. That speech was one of the most touching, dramatic, and from the heart speeches I've heard. It was very refreshing to hear someone come forth and talk about something that's really personal and hard to explain. I think we are really truly lucky to be able to hear a holocaust survivor and it really makes us think of how lucky we are. I do have to say I was really impressed on how humble and modest you were about how brave and hard working you were. I felt like such a small person in character in your presence because of how you explained how hate or revenge doesn't make you any better than those German who took your family who you loved so much. Thank you very much for teaching us those ever-so important lessons and I hope you have a happy life.

Sincerely,
Mikaela

Journal Entry #3

Powerful, moving, reality. These are three words that come into mind as I sit and contemplate Nate's speech. This is a man who has been through so much trying to forget everyday but simply cannot. On top of all of that, he then has the courage to stand in front of a room full of people who have never, and probably will never, experience anything like what he has and tell them his story. I could not imagine losing my family. They are THE most important thing in my life. I thank God for them and I could never imagine having to part with them. Nate's story makes us all open our eyes and really take a look at what happened during the Holocaust. It is easy for a person today to say that it was tragic that 6 million Jewish people died during World War II. It is not easy for most of those people to sit and listen to Nate tell his story. Over the course of my life, my family has never had large sums of money, but we have always had enough to live. I could not imagine living in the conditions of the concentration camp. The food and work and filth would seem unbearable. I am not apposed to an honest day of work, but this was awful. My eyes became wet when he talked of how he barely survived due to the fact that he was so short. How he was able to work so hard no one will ever know. It is truly inspirational to hear a man who has been through so much stand in front of you and speak so highly of a nation, the United States of America, that is always under so much criticism not only from outside, but from within. To hear him say, with water welling in his eyes, "God Bless America", sent a chill through me. As I stood to applaud, I felt as though Nate is a man who deserves this every day of his life. He should have a crowd following him wherever he goes to give him the recognition he deserves for persevering through so much. Compared to him, we are just simple people. Nate is a hero!!!

Dear Mr. Taffel,

Wow! Your speech at our school was really good. I liked it alot and it made me view not only the Holocaust but different people in general differently. Seeing your emotion and hearing your story gave me a new prospective on life. I thought that you would have wanted to get revenge on those horable people, but hearing you say that if you did you would be a killer just like them. Hearing you say that made me cry, and made me realize that we are all equal and there shouldn't be hate because of people's differences.

Sincerally,
Krissi [redacted]

Holocaust

By Kylie [redacted] and Hannah [redacted]

In World War II, the Holocaust,
Millions of innocent lives were lost.
Few survivors are left today,
And I was lucky and saw one anyway.

To concentration camps they went,
That is where some of their time was spent,
The rest of their time was spent doing chores,
And when they got back they had many sores.

The Unfortunate Jews were the first to go,
So the rest of the country tried to stay low.
But the Nazi's still came,
And to the disabled did the same.

Adolf Hitler started the war,
And because of it many families were tore.
Now, few survivors are left today,
And I was lucky and saw one anyway!

Dear Mr. Taffel,

Your speech was one of the most profound experiences that I have ever had. I never thought that I would see a real Holocaust survivor, and hearing your story was truly an honor. The courage that you must have to talk about such a horrendous experience after so many years of silence is absolutely amazing. The way that you were able to talk so freely about your family loss was so incredible. I am most definitely sorry for your losses, and I hope that you continue to tell your story because it is definitely one worth hearing. Thank you for your time, and good luck.

Sincerely,

Caroline [redacted]

St. Mary's Visitation

Excerpts From Letters

- "…thank you for teaching me something I never really thought about until you explained yourself. I will probably never forget that "hate destroys." That clicked in my head the moment you said it. I think that statement will stay in my mind the rest of my life …your speech not only influenced my life but I'm sure it found its way to others. So I encourage you to keep what you are doing. It does make a difference."

  – *Taylor*

- "I know you have had a hard time reliving it all — just to tell complete strangers how cruel life can get. I personally feel deeply sorry for what happened to you because my father is a German citizen. Most of my grandparents' families were involved with the war. The only reason I know as to why there were Nazis is because they were forced to join or be punished. My father's whole side of the family is very ashamed of how their nation treated you and all the other Jews … From your story, I have learned how one person's dream can just damn a whole race to hellish torments."

  – *Ben*

- "As you told your story, no one in the audience spoke a word. You intrigued everyone, helping them understand more than a textbook could teach us. Along with your story, came a message. Something that will stick forever in my mind is how strong the word hate is. It made me think of when I've said the word, and how misused it is. After you came to our school, I don't think I can ever use that word again. … You opened my eyes to what I have. With everything that happens in a teenager's life, I know I can be strong and know I am lucky for what I have. I know not to take things for granted, and to embrace life. I think I can speak for everyone when I say, keep spreading your story. I will never forget you, and I am thankful for what you taught me."

– Dani

- "I want to say that your words have inspired me. You are one of those people who come every once in a while, and will inspire millions. The strength that you showed and the courage you had made me realize that my life is not that bad. I am happy to say that after your presentation I went home a different person. I hugged my mother when she first walked in the door. I told my sister that I loved her."

– Jessica

- "I respect you and the fact that you are not a bitter, hateful person even though your experiences as a child were unimaginable. Listening to you tell your story made me teary at times. I have never gotten emotional during a school presentation before. I can't imagine living through what you have and still having the strength to see brighter days. For that, you are a hero. I will never forget your story. Someday, I will tell my children about you. Thank you so much for changing my outlook on hate and life in general."

– Stephanie

- "We can read about the Holocaust in textbooks, but being able to sit down and talk to a survivor and listen to all that you went through is the ultimate learning experience … It really touched me when you talked about how much you missed your family. We had to write about what we would miss the most if they were gone the next day and when you were talking about how you just got into the back of the truck and the cloth was laid over you and there were no goodbyes. I honestly can say I would never be able to do that. I give you a lot of credit for living with that fact because that would kill me."

– Abbi

- "When you came to the part in your presentation about not feeling any hatred towards the cruel people of Germany, I was simply amazed. I could not believe that a person who endured so many atrocious events could not be overcome with rage, and I felt so guilty for having hatred towards the tiniest things in my life. I cannot describe my gratitude towards you who has taught me in 60 minutes to enormously important life lessons – to not hate, and to love and cherish my family. You are the bravest, strongest and most inspiring person I have ever met and I promise that your story will remain with me for the rest of my life."

  – *Katie*

- "I was seated in the back of the auditorium as you spoke to our students and staff and I looked around at the students from time to time. Never have I been in the company of such a large crowd of ninth-graders sitting so attentively and quietly. From this alone, I know that my students heard your story. From our discussions in class the following day, I know it went to their hearts. It's hard to assess what big questions my students will leave our Holocaust studies with, but it is my greatest hope that the seeds of justice, peace and tolerance were planted. In many, I know they were. Your part in that, of course, was significant. For delving once again into your painful past for the hope of our youth and their futures, I thank you."

  – *Emily Goodrun*

Testimonials

How do you reach 12-year-olds in school? Difficult, even on our best days. But how do we teach them empathy and understanding for a terrible time that we can barely imagine? Movies, books and film clips offer a glimpse at the horror, but hearing Nate Taffel's testimony brings it alive.

Nate is "living history" and the students' lives are never quite the same after meeting him. His struggles and challenges remain in our hearts and souls long after their Holocaust projects have been completed, and long after one of his great big bear hugs. He lives on in every one of us, reminding us how important it is to truly live, to value education and our families, and to be proud to live in such a wonderful, free country.

Most importantly, he inspires us to carry with us the secret of life: to treat others the way we wish to be treated.

We can reach these young minds, the ones that, in the near future, will be running our country. Nate reminds them that terrible things can happen again . . . "The only thing necessary for evil to triumph is for good people to do nothing." Never forget.

Linda Lee Weiner
Kennedy Middle School
Germantown, WI

Nate Taffel's quietly riveting story of his youth is absolutely mesmerizing; my students are literally on the edges of their seats. Afterward, they leave with a sense of humility and hope.

Mr. Taffel relays his story with directness and simplicity; through his words, my students gain an understanding of the differences between life and death, love and hate, tolerance and intolerance all in one sitting.

I have never seen my students so utterly mesmerized as they were hearing Nate Taffel's story. Afterwards, they couldn't wait to meet him, thank him, shake his hand or hug him. To many, Mr. Taffel is their hero.

Students and staff alike were absolutely transformed forever in hearing Nate Taffel's poignant story of his youth. Afterwards, students pledged to remove the word "hate" from their vocabulary.

Many of my former students come back to tell me that experiencing Nate Taffel's compelling story is the highlight of their educational career; Mr. Taffel's powerful and affecting story and message is woven into their hearts forever.

"Upon hearing Mr. Taffel's heartbreaking reality of his youth, my students whole-heartedly connect to him and put the pieces together. They realize they have a huge responsibility — that they are the world's next generation of witnesses. Mr. Taffel's words stay with them and they are motivated to act and speak without hate and intolerance.

Beth Larson
Menomonee Falls High School
Menomonee Falls, WI

About the author:

Keri Guten Cohen was born in Milwaukee and grew up in Dallas. She graduated from the University of Texas at Austin with degrees in journalism and history. She worked as a reporter and features editor for daily newspapers in Beaumont and San Antonio, Texas, and Dayton, Ohio, before coming to the *Detroit Jewish News,* a weekly newsmagazine where she is story development editor. She lives in West Bloomfield, Mich., with her husband Don and daughters Hannah and Emma. She talks to her Uncle Nate every week.